Engineering in My Community

Robin Johnson

CRABTREE
PUBLISHING COMPANY
WWW.CRABTREEBOOKS.COM

Title-Specific Learning Objectives:

Readers will:
- Identify some ways that engineers make life in a community easier, safer, and more fun.
- Make text-to-self connections by identifying some solutions in their own community.
- Ask and answer questions about main ideas in the text.

High-frequency words (grade one) a, an, and, are, in, is, play, the, use	Academic vocabulary creative, design, escalator, fire extinguisher, ramp, solutions, solve, tools, travel

Before, During, and After Reading Prompts:

Activate Prior Knowledge and Make Predictions:

Have children read the title and look at the cover and title-page images. Make a KWL chart and fill in the "Know" and "Want to Know" sections. Ask:

- What is engineering? What do engineers do?
- What do you already know about engineering in our community?
- What do you want to know about engineering in our community?

During Reading:

After reading pages 4 and 5, ask children:

- What are the main ideas on this page? Do they help answer any of the questions on our chart?

- Can you explain what an engineer is, in your own words?
- What do engineers do? What do they design? (Note that engineers design solutions that make life easier, safer, and more fun.)

Repeat this process after reading pages 6 and 7, to connect to questions about communities.

After Reading:

Fill in the "Learned" section of the KWL chart. Encourage children to share what they learned after reading. They should answer questions or flesh out ideas that appear in their "Want to Know" section. Create an anchor chart with key concepts and child-created definitions.

Author: Robin Johnson

Series Development: Reagan Miller

Editor: Janine Deschenes

Proofreader: Melissa Boyce

STEAM Notes for Educators: Janine Deschenes

Guided Reading Leveling: Publishing Solutions Group

Cover, Interior Design, and Prepress: Samara Parent

Photo research: Robin Johnson and Samara Parent

Production coordinator: Katherine Berti

Photographs:
iStock: recep-bg: p. 7 (bottom); fishwork: p. 11 (left)
All other photographs by Shutterstock

Library and Archives Canada Cataloguing in Publication

Johnson, Robin (Robin R.), author
    Engineering in my community / Robin Johnson.

(Full STEAM ahead!)
Includes index.
Issued in print and electronic formats.
ISBN 978-0-7787-6205-8 (hardcover).--
ISBN 978-0-7787-6250-8 (softcover).--ISBN 978-1-4271-2261-2 (HTML)

    1. Civil engineering--Juvenile literature. 2. Municipal engineering-
-Juvenile literature. 3. Cities and towns--Juvenile literature. I. Title.

TA149.J64 2019   j624   C2018-906168-5
                                            C2018-906169-3

Library of Congress Cataloging-in-Publication Data

Names: Johnson, Robin (Robin R.) author.
Title: Engineering in my community / Robin Johnson.
Description: New York, New York : Crabtree Publishing Company, 2019.
  | Series: Full STEAM ahead! | Includes index.
Identifiers: LCCN 2018056591 (print) | LCCN 2018059401 (ebook) |
  ISBN 9781427122612 (Electronic) |
  ISBN 9780778762058 (hardcover : alk. paper) |
  ISBN 9780778762508 (pbk. : alk. paper)
Subjects: LCSH: Engineering--Juvenile literature.
Classification: LCC TA149 (ebook) | LCC TA149 .J64 2019 (print) |
  DDC 620--dc23
LC record available at https://lccn.loc.gov/2018056591

Printed in the U.S.A./042019/CG20190215

Table of Contents

Crabtree Publishing Company
www.crabtreebooks.com   1-800-387-7650

Published in Canada
Crabtree Publishing
616 Welland Ave.
St. Catharines, Ontario
L2M 5V6

Published in the United States
Crabtree Publishing
PMB 59051
350 Fifth Avenue, 59th Floor
New York, New York 10118

Published in the United Kingdom
Crabtree Publishing
Maritime House
Basin Road North, Hove
BN41 1WR

Published in Australia
Crabtree Publishing
Unit 3 – 5 Currumbin Court
Capalaba
QLD 4157

What is an Engineer?

An engineer is a person who uses math, science, and **creative thinking** to solve problems. Engineers **design** solutions that we use every day.

fire extinguisher

Engineers design solutions that make life safer.
A fire extinguisher helps us stop fires.

alarm clock

Engineers design solutions
that make life easier.
An alarm clock helps us
wake up on time.

in-line skates

Engineers design solutions
that make life more fun.
In-line skates help us
have fun outside.

In Your Community

Engineers solve problems in communities.
A community is a group of people who
live, work, and play in a place.
Your school, home, and neighborhood
are communities.

Engineers design things that solve problems and meet
needs in communities.

Engineers help farmers in your community grow food for you to eat.

Engineers give you clean water to drink in your community.

Building Communities

There are big and small buildings in your community. Engineers design them all! They make sure the buildings meet the needs of the people in a community.

Some buildings reach up to the sky! They were designed for crowded cities. They take up less space, but can fit many people.

Engineers design school buildings that give students the space to learn.

ramp

Engineers design buildings with ramps. The ramps let people who use wheelchairs enter the buildings.

Home Sweet Home

Engineers design the houses in your community. They also design things that you use in your home and yard each day.

Engineers design houses to solve the problem of where people will live.

washing machine

shovel

Engineers design
washing machines
that make it easier
to clean our clothes.

Engineers design
shovels that help
people move
heavy snow.

11

School Tools

Engineers design tools that let you learn and play in your school community.

A pencil is a tool you use at school. A desk is a school tool too! What other tools do you see in this picture?

pencil

desk

Engineers design **computers** to help us do work.

Engineers design school playgrounds that let everyone have fun.

From Place to Place

You **travel** in your community. Some people bike or walk to the park. Some people take the bus or ride in a car to school. Engineers design things that help you travel.

scooter

backpack

Engineers design scooters that make traveling more fun. They design backpacks to make it easier to carry things.

14

Engineers design school buses that make it easier for students to travel to school.

Engineers design lights that tell you when it is safe to cross roads.

Safe Travel

Engineers design ways to make traveling safer. Look around your community. What solutions keep you safe when you travel?

Engineers design bridges. They let people or cars cross safely over water.

guardrail

helmet →

child seat

Engineers design guardrails that make roads safer. They stop cars from going off the roads.

Engineers design child seats. They keep children safe when they ride on bicycles. Engineers design helmets that keep us safe too.

Community Helpers

There are many helpers in your community. Police and firefighters help keep you safe. Doctors and nurses help keep you healthy. Engineers design the **tools** that these community helpers use.

Police use tools to check how fast cars are going. They make sure people are driving safely.

Engineers design fire trucks. They design hoses and other tools that help firefighters put out fires.

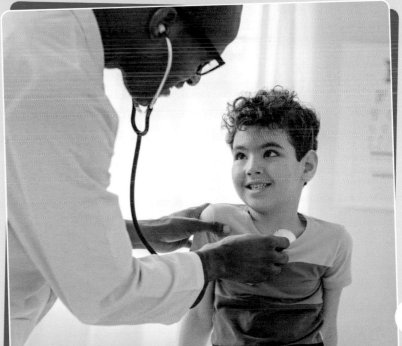

Doctors use tools to check things like your heartbeat.

Engineering All Around

Look around your community. You will see engineers' solutions everywhere you go!

Engineers design easier ways to **sort** trash.
They help people decide which things to **recycle**.

Engineers design escalators. They make it easy for people to move up and down.

escalator

Engineers design ways to make grocery shopping easier! They design carts to carry the food.

21

Words to Know

computers [kuh m-PYOO-ters] noun Electronic devices that do jobs

creative thinking [kree-EY-tiv THING-king] noun Using your mind to make up new and original ideas

design [dih-ZAHYN] verb To make a plan for how something is made or built

needs [needs] noun Things people require to live, such as water

recycle [ree-SAHY-kuh l] verb To make used items into something new

sort [sawrt] verb To put things that are alike in groups

tools [tools] noun Devices that help us do work

travel [TRAV-uh l] verb To move from one place to another

A noun is a person, place, or thing.

A verb is an action word that tells you what someone or something does.

An adjective is a word that tells you what something is like.

Index

About the Author

Robin Johnson is a freelance author and editor who has written more than 80 children's books. When she isn't working, Robin builds castles in the sky with her engineer husband and their two best creations—sons Jeremy and Drew.

To explore and learn more, enter the code at the Crabtree Plus website below.

www.crabtreeplus.com/fullsteamahead

Your code is:
fsa20

STEAM Notes for Educators

Full STEAM Ahead is a literacy series that helps readers build vocabulary, fluency, and comprehension while learning about big ideas in STEAM subjects. *Engineering in My Community* allows readers to ask and answer questions about main ideas by clearly repeating key concepts and encouraging text-to-self connections. The STEAM activity below helps readers extend the ideas in the book to build their skills in arts and engineering.

We Need Engineering!

Children will be able to:
- Explore their community to find engineering solutions.
- Create a poster that shows how we need engineering in our community.

Materials
- Exploring My Community Worksheet
- Poster board and tools such as markers, rulers, crayons, stencils, etc.

Guiding Prompts
After reading *Engineering in My Community*, ask:
- Can you think of ways engineers make life easier, safer, and more fun?
- Look around the classroom. Can you find something that an engineer designed? Does it make learning easier, safer, or more fun?

Activity Prompts
Review the definition of community on page 6:
- A group of people who live, work, and play in a place. Your school, home, and neighborhood are all communities.

Hand each child an Exploring My Community Worksheet. Explain that they will make observations in their home, school, and neighborhood to identify engineering solutions.

First, take a walk around the school and model making some observations of solutions. Together, fill in the "school" section of the worksheet. Then, children should take the worksheet home and fill in the "home" and "neighborhood" sections. Educators should notify parents about the activity prior to assigning this "homework."

When worksheets are completed, children will use the information they gathered to create "We Need Engineering!" posters. The posters will:
- Show some of the engineering solutions we rely on in our community.
- Include the title: We Need Engineering!
- Include three sections for the three "communities" explored: home, school, neighborhood.
- Include three to five pictures of solutions that they found in each "community."

Extensions
- Invite children to choose one school solution and prepare a short presentation describing why it is important in their school community.

To view and download the worksheet, visit **www.crabtreebooks.com/resources/printables** or **www.crabtreeplus.com/fullsteamahead** and enter the code **fsa20**.